Vol 6

MAZE

Ages 4-6

FOR KIDS

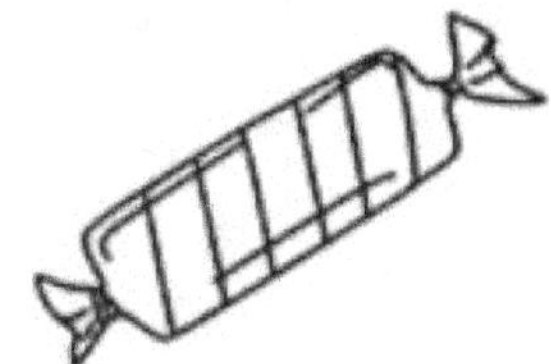

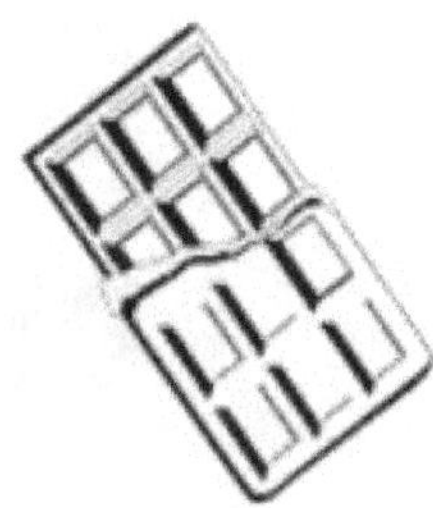

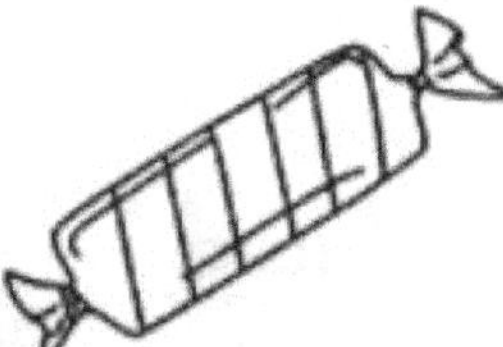

MAZE BOOK

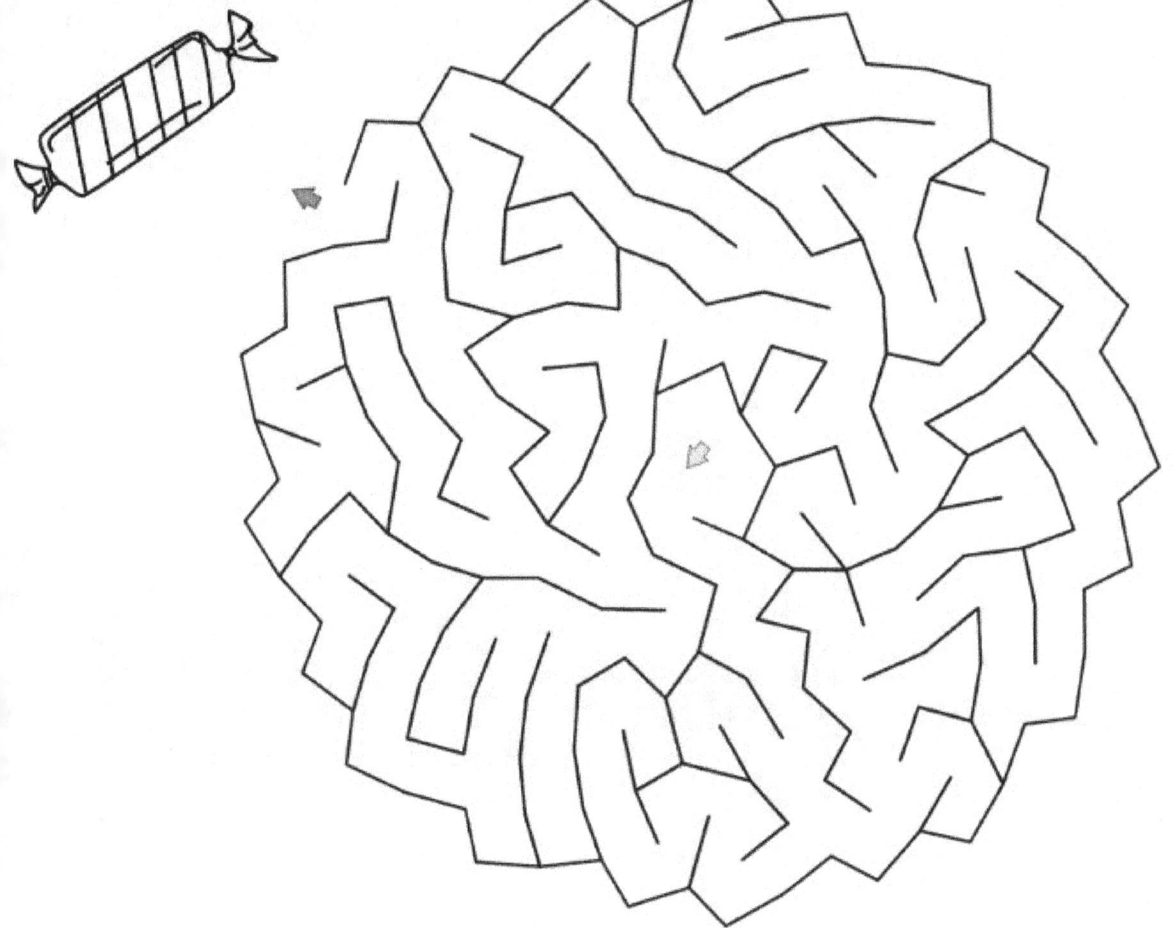

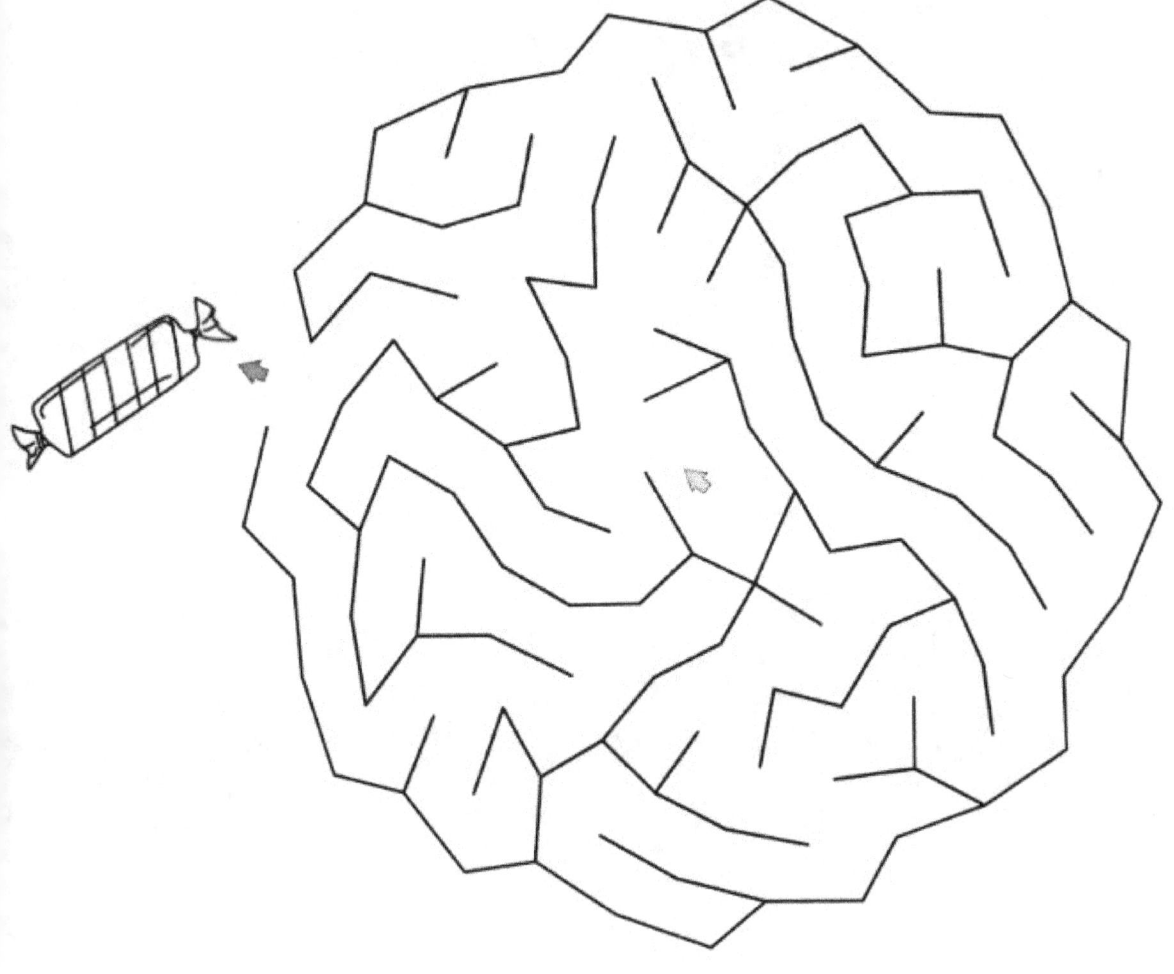

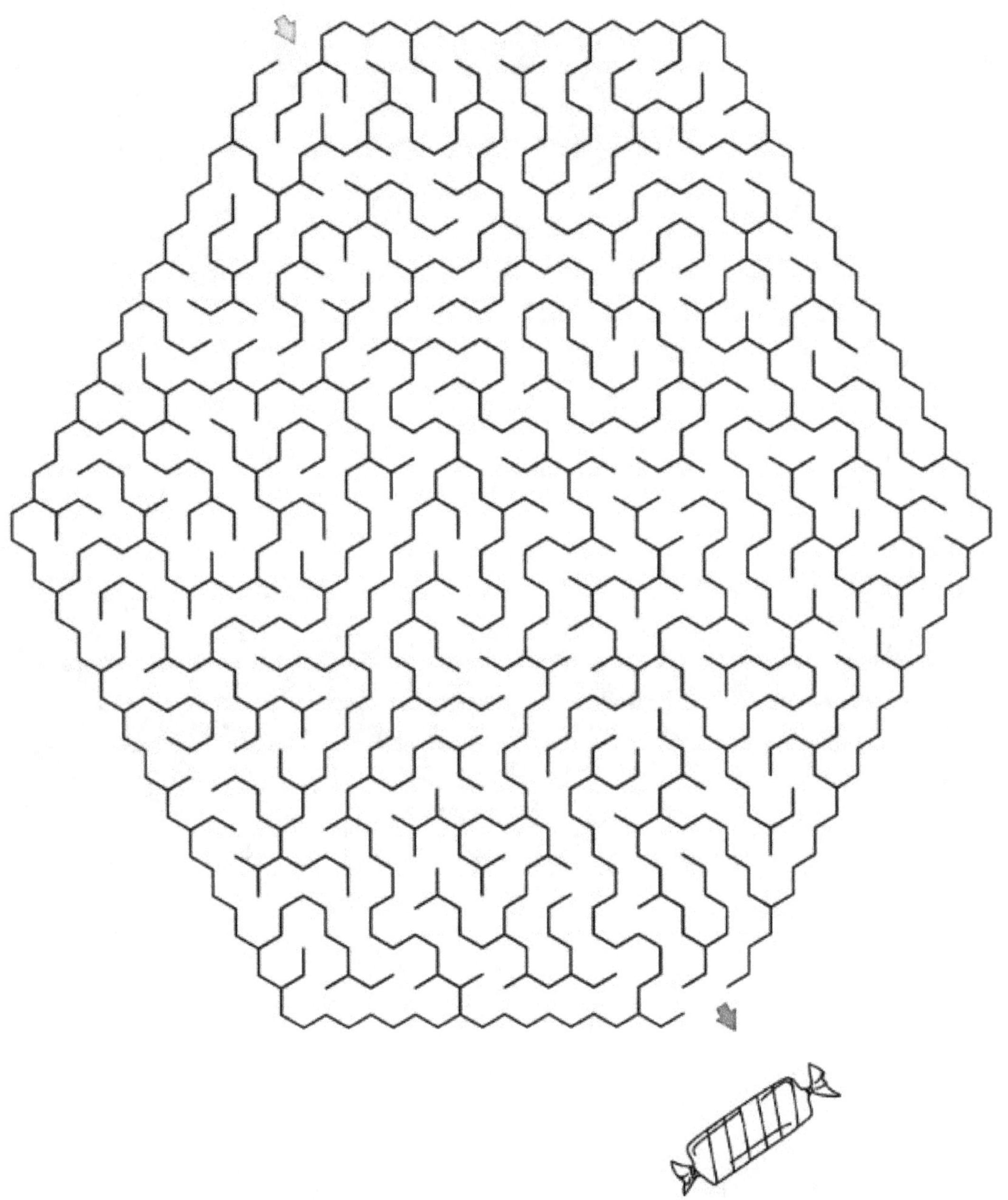

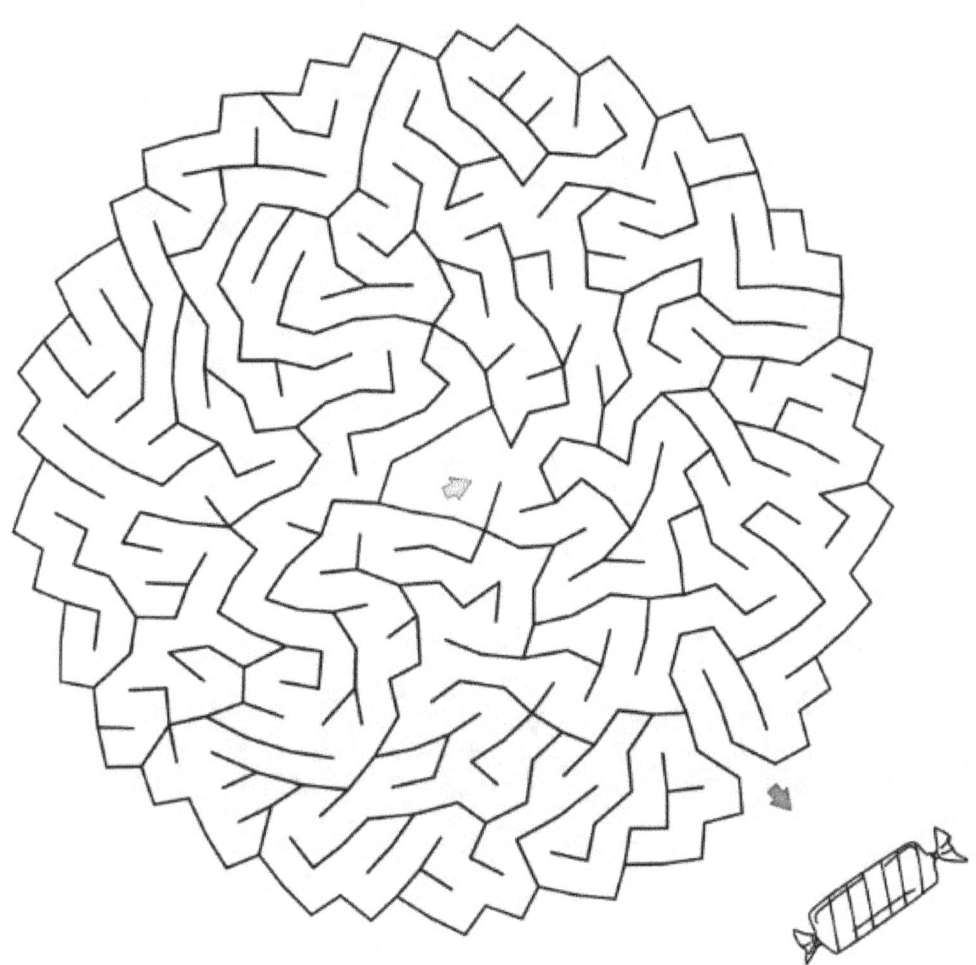

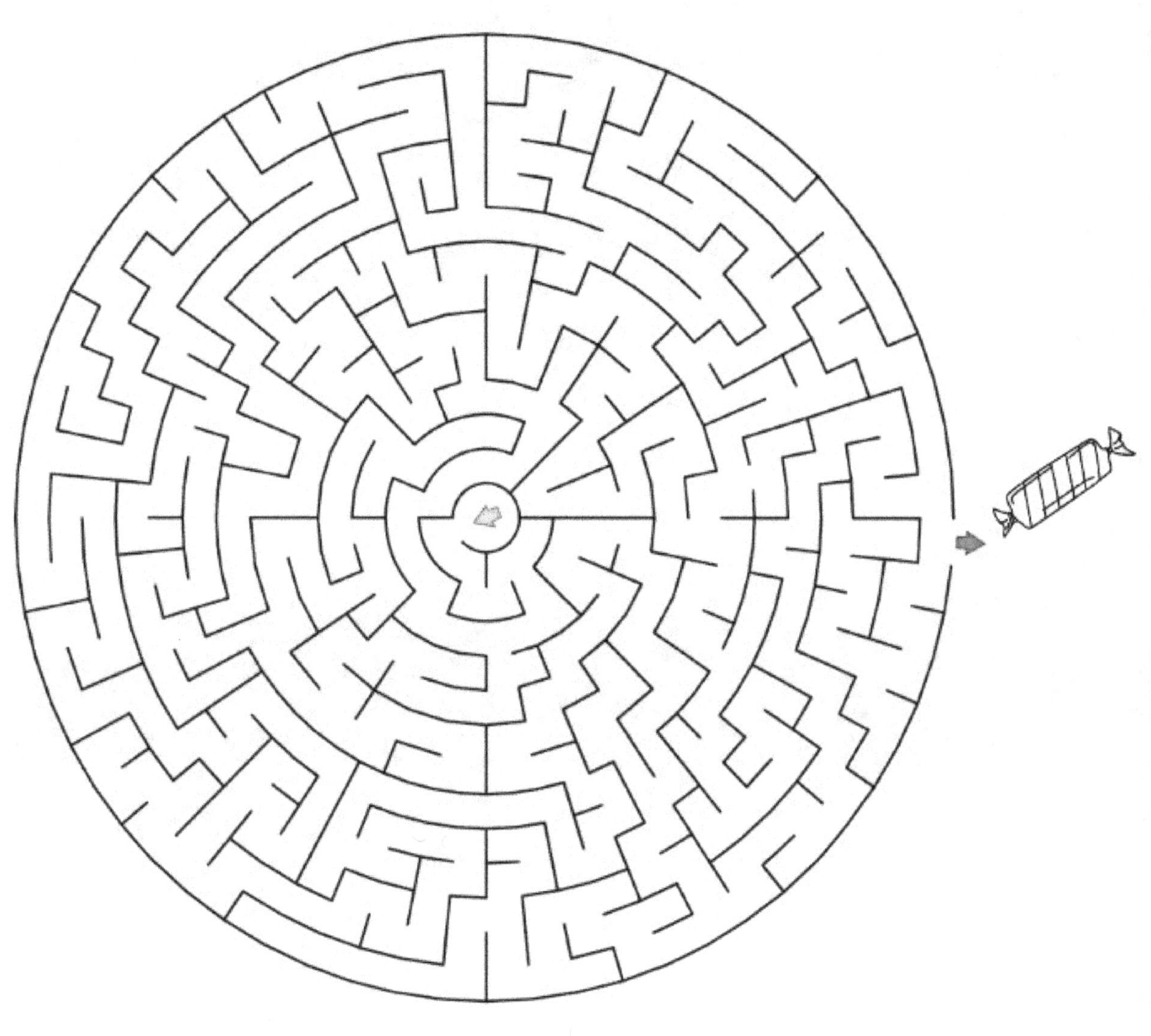

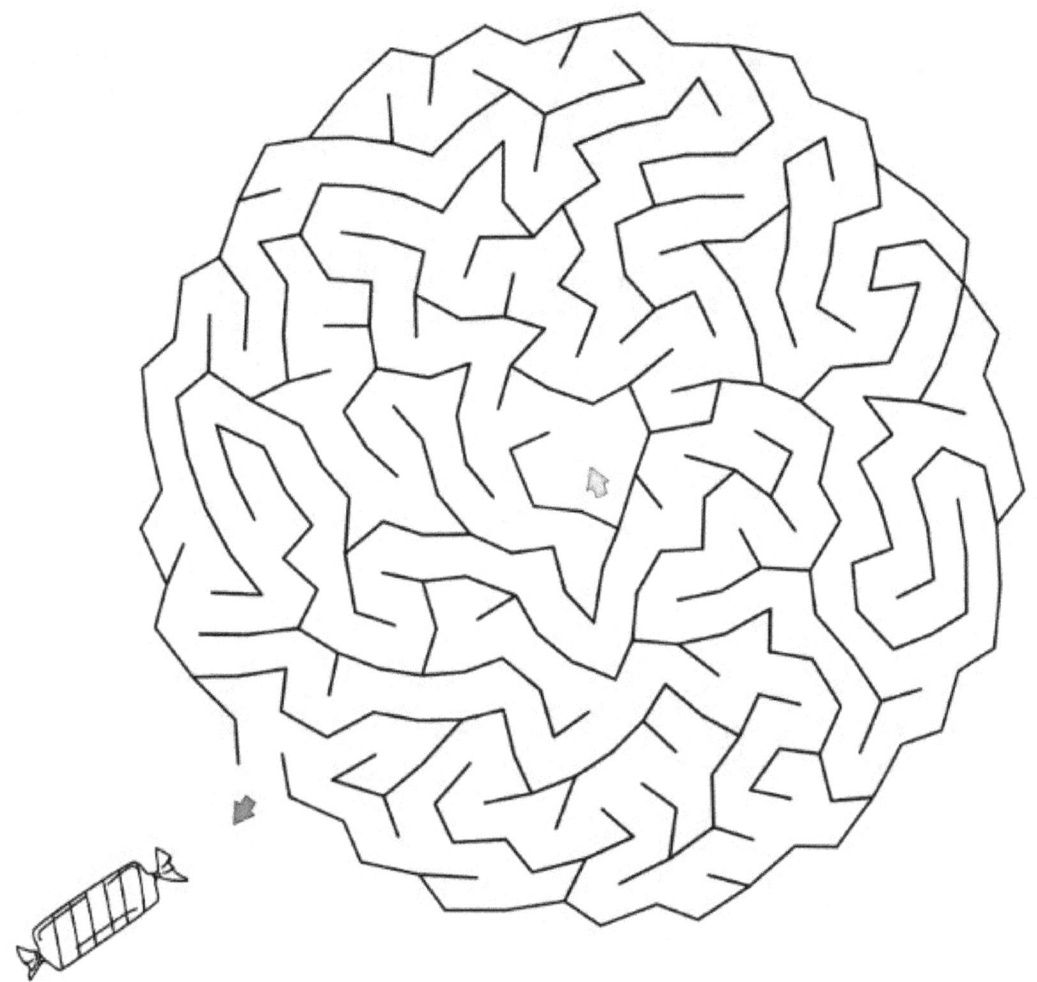

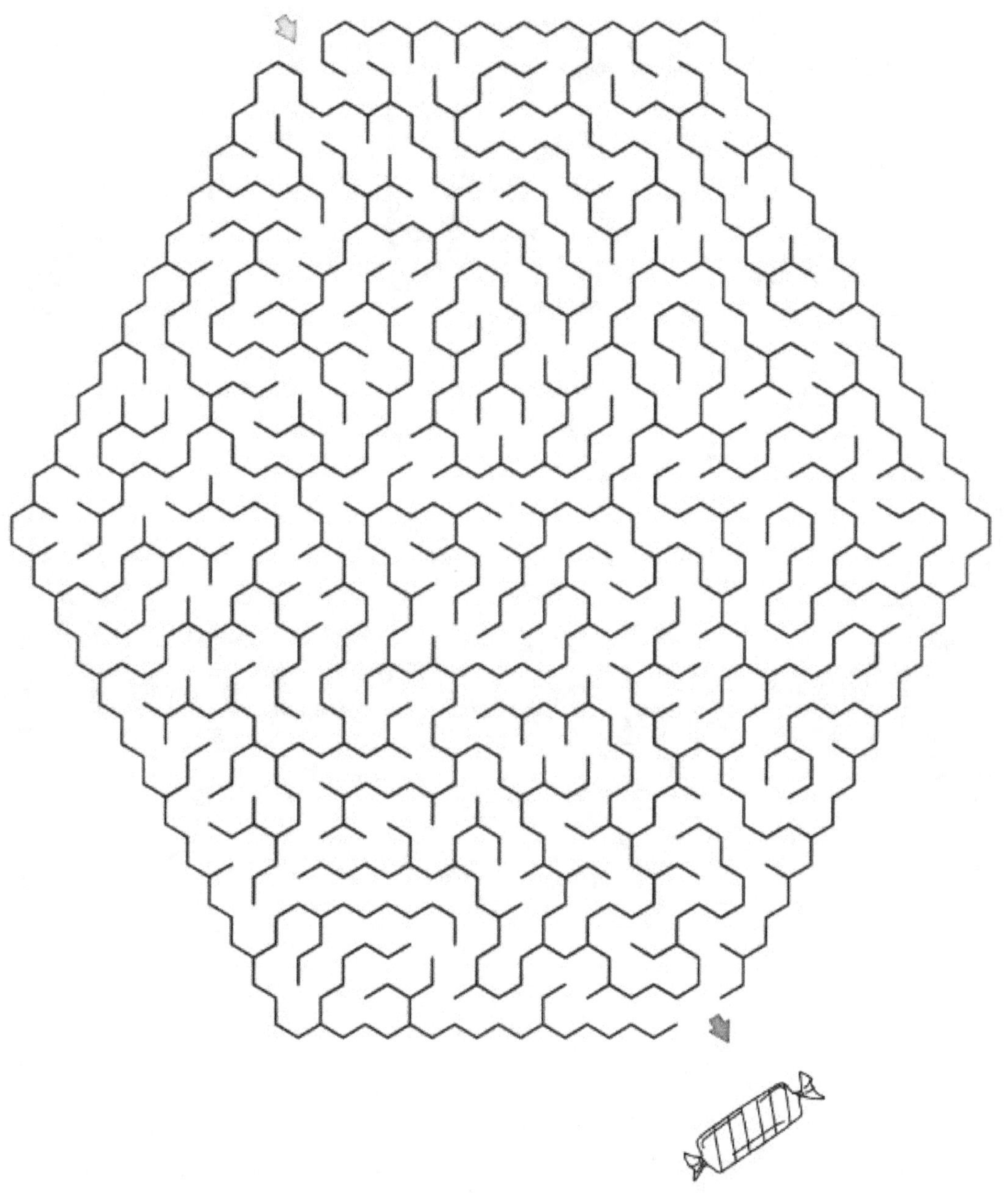

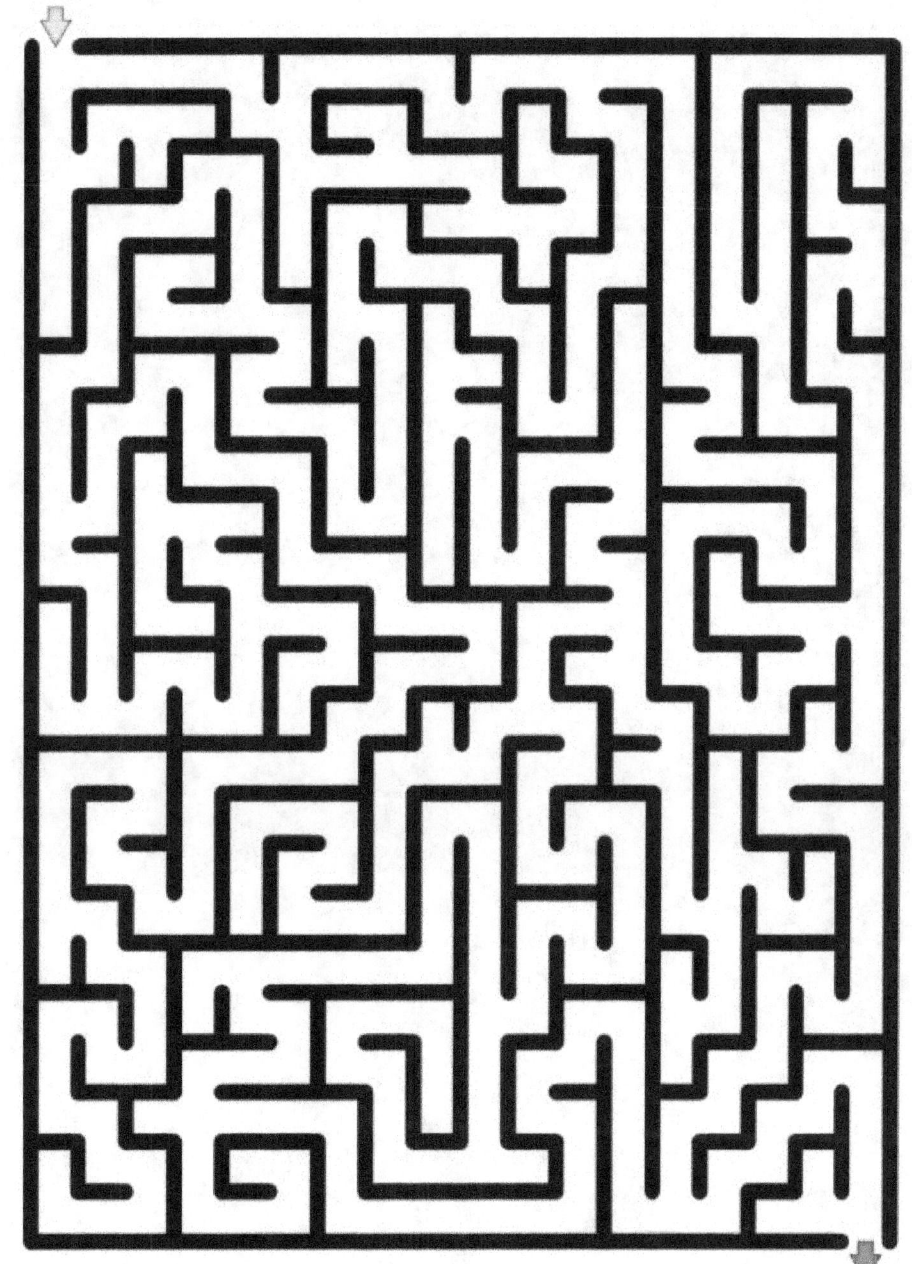

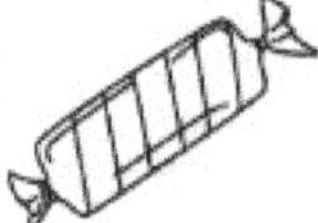

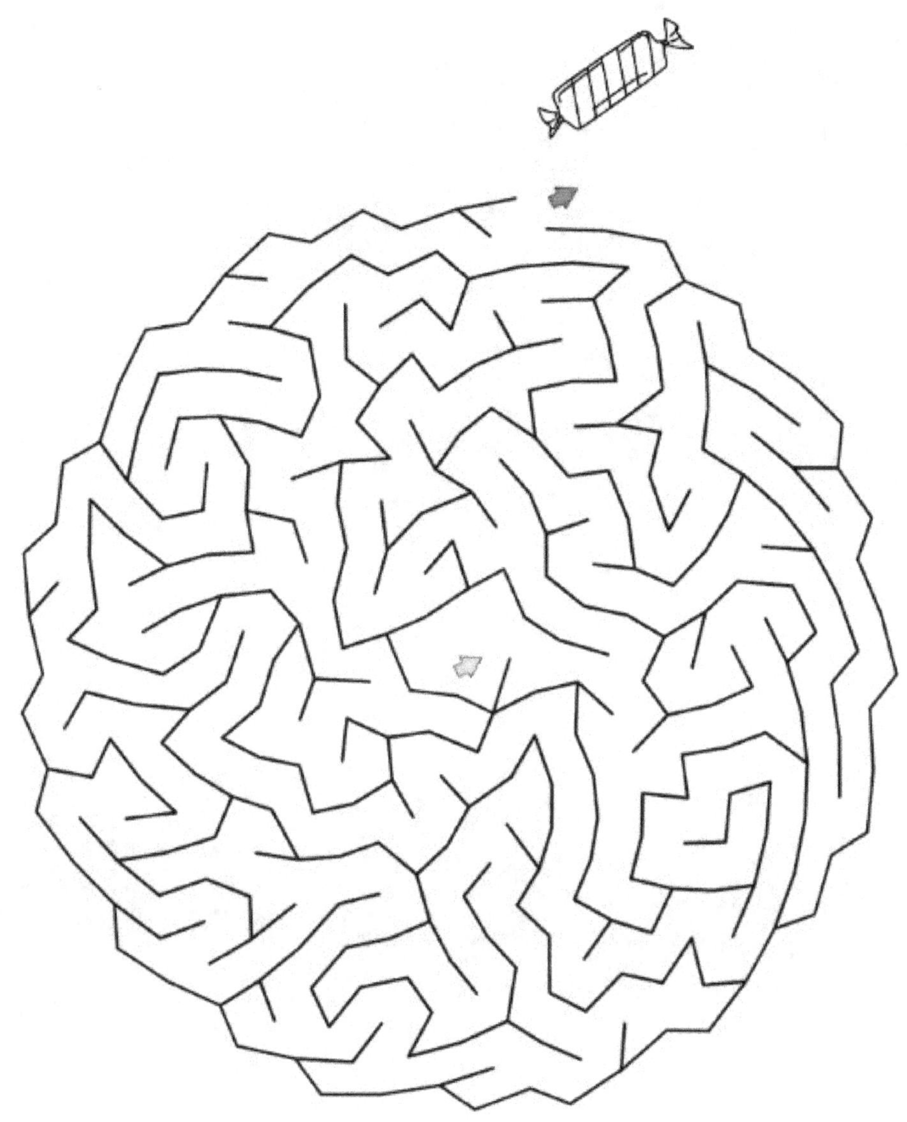

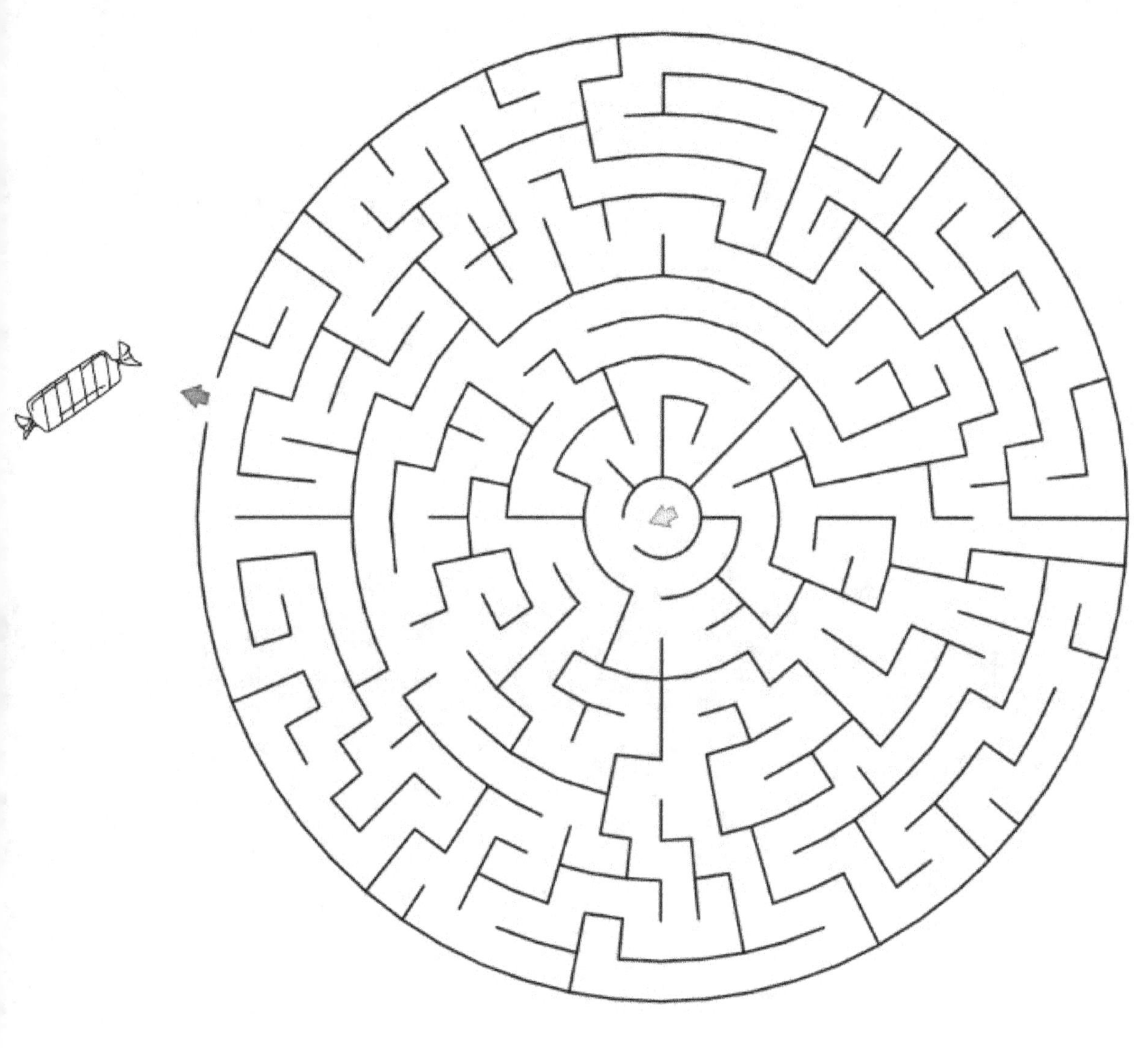

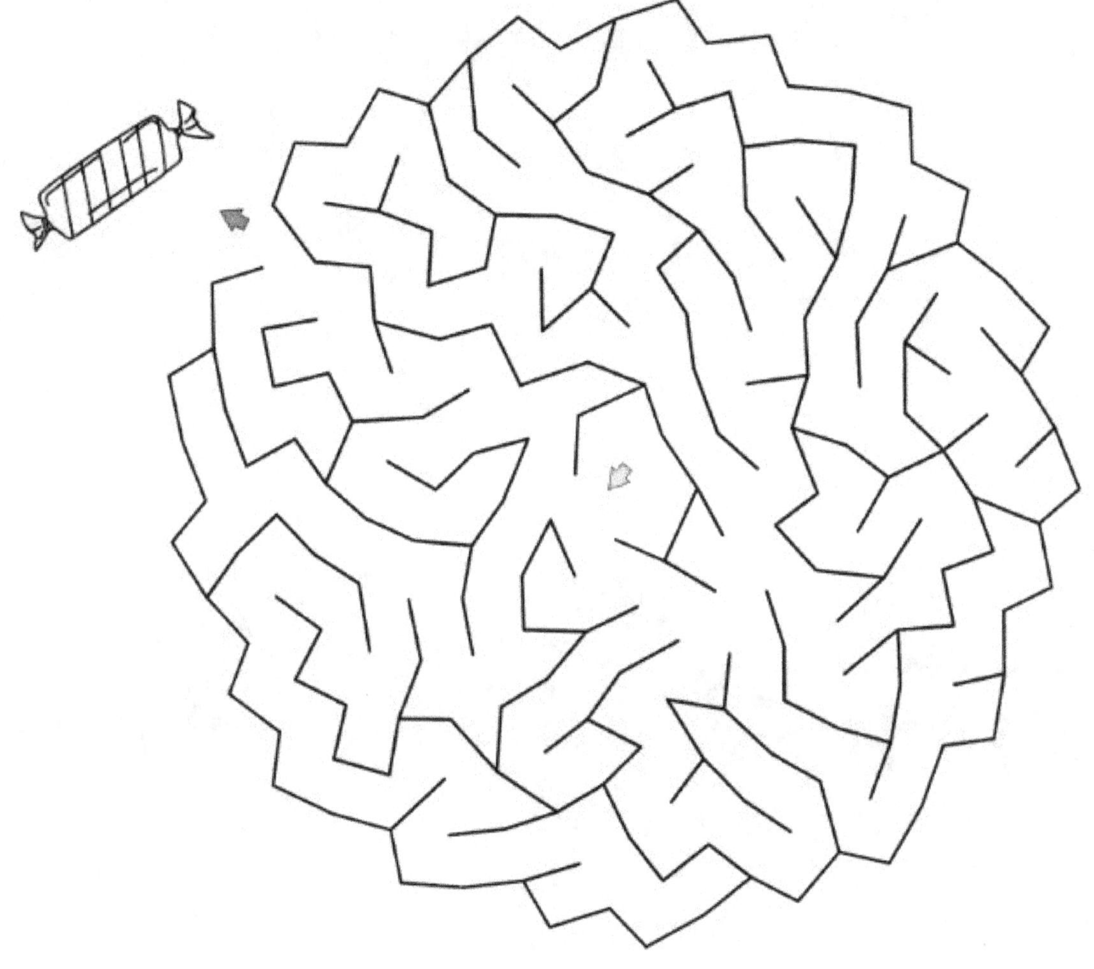

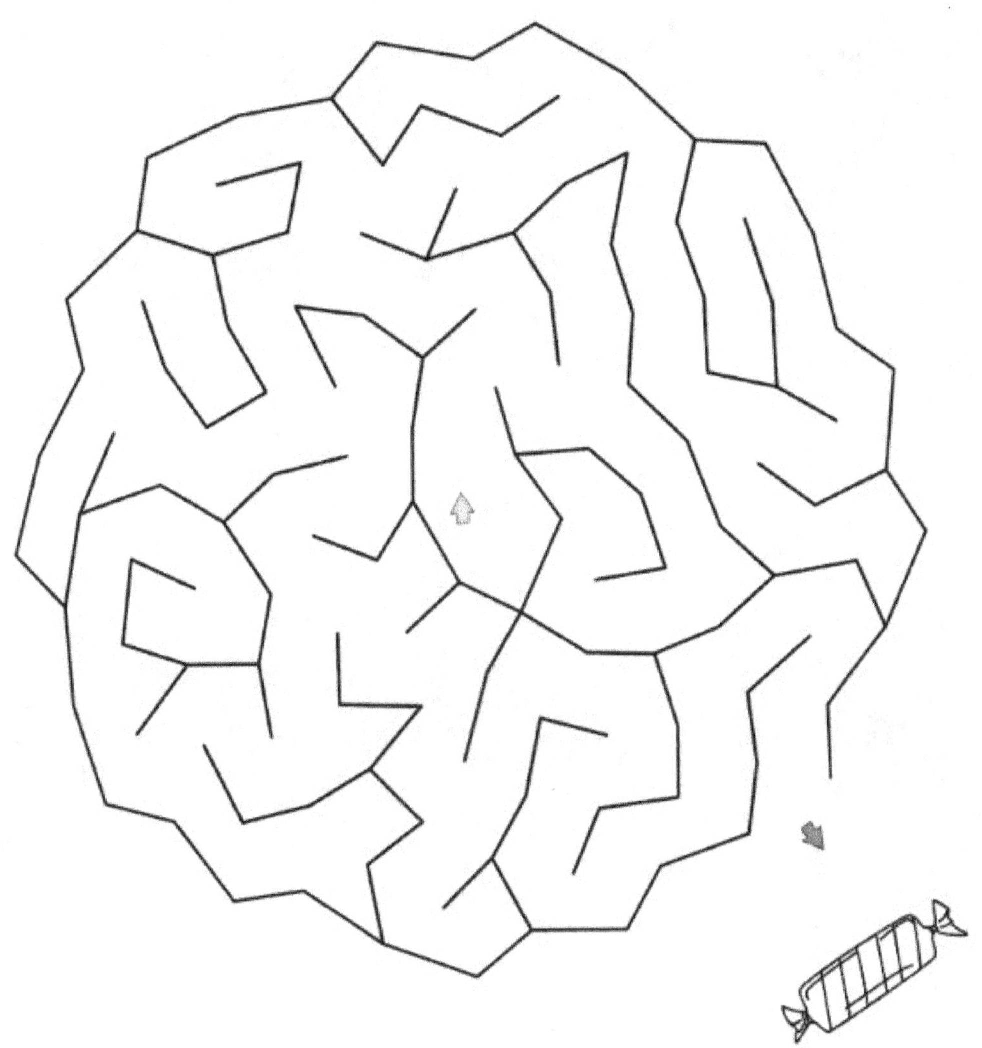